Roads Take Us Home

Roads Take Us Home

a building block book

Lee Sullivan Hill

Carolrhoda Books, Inc./Minneapolis

To my Goshen, CT, writing friends: Louise, Nancy, and Becky. Thanks!
—L. S. H.

The photographs in this book are reproduced through the courtesy of: D. J. Lambrecht, front cover; Paula Borchardt, back cover, pp. 10, 19; Tony LaGruth, pp. 1, 16; Howard Ande, pp. 2, 14, 23, 25; James Marshall, pp. 5, 6, 15, 24; Paul T. McMahon, p. 7; Jerry Hennen, pp. 8, 29; Visuals Unlimited, pp. 9 (Steve McCutcheon), 20 (Terry C. Hazen), 21 (Mark E. Gibson); Don Eastman, p. 11; James P. Rowan, p. 12; Bob Firth, pp. 13, 28; Douglas Steakley, p. 17; Erwin C. "Bud" Neilsen, "Images International," p. 22; Cheryl Koenig Morgan, p. 26; Betty Crowell, p. 27.

Carolrhoda Books, Inc. c/o The Lerner Group
241 First Avenue North, Minneapolis, MN 55401

Library of Congress Cataloging-in-Publication Data

Hill, Lee Sullivan, 1958–
   Roads take us home / by Lee Sullivan Hill.
     p.   cm. — (A Building block book)
   Includes index.
   Summary: An introduction to the variety and beauty of American roads, past and present.
   ISBN 1-57505-022-6
   1. Roads—United States—Juvenile literature. 2. Roads—United States—History—Juvenile literature. I. Title. II. Series.
TE149.H55 1997   96-11639

Manufactured in the United States of America
1 2 3 4 5 6 SP 02 01 00 99 98 97

Roads follow rivers. They cut through
city parks. Roads take you places like your
grandma's house or school.

Ride down a road and open the window. Take
a deep breath. What do you smell?

This street smells of wet leaves and slush.

Winter is in the air!

Native Americans traveled the first roads
in North America. They followed deer paths
through the woods. Pioneers turned those same
paths into dirt roads for their wagons.

To keep their wagon wheels from sinking, pioneers put logs in the wet spots. They laid logs side by side.

The road looked like corduroy: bump-low, bump-low, all in a row. Pioneers called the log roads "corduroy roads."

City builders used round stones instead of logs to pave streets. You can still see cobblestones on Prince Street in Alexandria, Virginia.

Most roads are built to last. Over 2,000 years ago, Romans built a stone road called the Appian Way. It still runs from Rome to Brindisi, Italy.

Other roads don't last after people stop using them. Wagons once followed the Oregon Trail. Now the wagons and the roads have all but disappeared.

Is your road old or new? What is its name?
Some roads, like Washington Street, are named
after a person. How about Rocky Road? Or
Spaghetti Junction?

Some roads have numbers. Route 66 runs
east and west. You can follow it from Illinois
to California and back again.

Route 1 runs north and south. It goes all the
way from Maine to Florida.

Highways like Route 1 take you where you
need to go. But superhighways like Route 80 are
even faster. They have no red lights. Ramps help
drivers get on and off the road.

Highways are straight. Other roads twist and turn. Lombard Street can make you dizzy. It's the most crooked street in San Francisco.

The Santa Monica Freeway is another
California road. It's long and straight and
ten lanes wide.

An earthquake ripped the road apart in 1994. It was closed for months. Finally, workers finished the repairs. Once again, millions of cars and trucks travel the Santa Monica Freeway.

Before a road is built or rebuilt, engineers plan. First they test the dirt by making mud pies. Some kinds of dirt are stronger than others. Can this dirt hold up a new road?

Engineers do more tests back in the lab. After all the tests, they draw plans for the new road. Then surveyors mark where the road will go.

Teams of workers and machines build the road. High spots are cut down. Low spots are filled up. Bulldozers push the dirt. Sheepsfoot rollers pack it down. Finally, the roadbed is flat and straight.

Dump trucks bring stones to spread over the roadbed. Graders make the road smooth. Then paving machines cover the road with concrete.

A highway crew in Israel just finished
repaving this road. Are you ready for a ride?

Highway crews work hard to keep roads safe. They repave roads and patch potholes. They hook up plows to their orange trucks and clear away snow.

Have you ever built a road for toy trucks to travel? When you grow up, you could build a real road.

You could become an engineer and plan roads.
You could drive a bulldozer and make roads flat
and straight. Or you could work on a highway
crew and ride around in an orange truck.

Next time you read about Little Red Riding Hood on the path to her grandma's house, think about roads. Roads take us to faraway places, family, and friends.

Then roads take us back home again.

A Photo Index to the Roads in This Book

Cover A rainbow lights the sky over U.S. Highway 89. This road leads to the Museum of the Plains Indian in Montana.

Page 1 Routes 4 and 12 meet in Woodstock, Vermont. There are flowers in the middle of the intersection. Roads are often decorated with flowers, flags, or banners.

Page 2 This road winds through a park in Connecticut. If you're quiet, you can hear the rushing water of the Housatonic River.

Page 5 A school bus carries children down Irving Street in Poughkeepsie, New York. Do you ride a bus to school?

Page 6 It smells of Chinese food on Canal Street in New York City.

Page 7 The first snow has dusted Gately Terrace in Madison, Wisconsin. Did you notice that this road is called a terrace? Road names can end with road, street, terrace, place, lane, avenue, highway, and many other words.

Page 8 Some paths have become roads. Luckily, others, like this one, have stayed wild for us to enjoy. Here people can hike through Antos Woods in Illinois.

Page 9 This corduroy road is in Alaska. Dirt and mud filled in the cracks between the logs.

Page 10 Prince Street in Old Town Alexandria has round cobblestones. Different cities used different kinds of paving stones, from round stones (like these) to square granite blocks to red bricks. Have you heard of the Yellow Brick Road?

Page 11 Appius Claudius Caecus was in charge of building the Appian Way. It is named after him. Traces of Roman roads can be found all over Western Europe, as far north as England.

Page 12 These wheel marks are found at the Oregon Trail Ruts National Historic Landmark in Guernsey, Wyoming. The Oregon Trail led pioneers to new lands in the West. After railroads opened up a faster way to travel, the wagon trains stopped.

Page 13 Where freeways and highways cross, people often give the roads the nickname "Spaghetti Junction." From above, these highways in Minneapolis, Minnesota, really do look like strands of spaghetti.

Page 14 Route 66 in Kingman, Arizona, shines during a pause in a thunderstorm. Older highways have motels, restaurants, and sign after sign, right along the roadside.

Page 15 Route 1 runs through Wiscasset, Maine. Why is it called Route *1*? In 1921, the U.S. Congress passed a Federal Highway Act. Route 1 was the first federal highway, so it got the first number.

Page 16 Interstate 80 goes all the way from the East to the West Coast. These ten lanes in New Jersey are divided into sections for "cars only" and for "trucks and cars." Concrete barriers and grassy median strips keep the vehicles apart. Divided highways and ramps make it safer to travel on crowded roads.

Page 17 Lombard Street is also called Snake Alley. Can you see why?

Pages 18 and 19 The Santa Monica Freeway has both a name and a number. It is also called U.S. Highway 10.

In January 1994, the Northridge Earthquake wrecked the Santa Monica Freeway. With crews working day and night, the freeway reopened by mid-April.

Page 20 An engineer in South Carolina is studying dirt where a road will be built. A steel tube hooked onto a drill took this dirt sample from deep underground. If you like to dig in the dirt, you could be a soils engineer when you grow up.

 **Page 21** This surveyor, called the crew chief, uses a tool called a theodolite (thee-AH-duhl-ite). The theodolite is aimed at the chief's helper, who stands where the new road belongs. The chief looks through the theodolite and yells to his helper to move left or right. When his helper stands in just the right spot, the chief will yell, "Good!" A bright ribbon on a wooden stake will mark the spot for the bulldozers to begin work.

 **Page 22** An excavator can scoop up *lots* of dirt with its huge bucket. Then the loader can quickly move the dirt into a dump truck. See the surveyor in the lower right corner?

 **Page 23** A new road will soon cross over Route 20 in Hammond, Indiana.

 **Page 24** This road is in the Negev Desert of Israel. From way up high, the road looks like a serpent in the sand.

 **Page 25** A truck with its snowplow attached clears New Lebanon Road in Hampshire, Illinois. *Katy &*

the Big Snow, by Virginia Lee Burton, tells a story about clearing snowy roads.

 **Page 26** In Miami, Florida, a boy drives his truck along the edge of a playground. You could make a road in a sandbox or in your bedroom out of blocks. Where else can you build a road?

 **Page 27** This worker for Caltrans (short for the California Department of Transportation) holds a sign that says "slow" on one side and "stop" on the other. He directs drivers around roadwork.

 Page 28 Out West, roads run for miles without a curve or a hill. It looks as if this highway runs right into heaven.

 **Page 29** This driveway leads to a home not far from Chicago, Illinois. What kind of road takes *you* home?